Nature's Children

ARMADILLOS

Amanda Harman

GROLIER

FACTS IN BRIEF

Classification of Armadillos

Class: *Mammalia* (mammals)
Order: *Xenarthra* (used to be Edentata, "toothless" mammals)
Family: *Dasypodidae* (armadillos)
Genus: There are 8 genera of armadillos.
Species: There are 20 species of armadillos.

World distribution.   Throughout South America, Central America, and the southern United States.

Habitat.   Different species live in different habitats, from forests through scrubland and deserts to savanna.

Distinctive physical characteristics.   Tough armor made up of bands of thick bony scales, and a small, pointed head with upright ears.

Habits.   Spend most of their time alone, foraging for food at night and sleeping in dug-out burrows during the day.

Diet.   Insects such as ants and termites or beetles, spiders, worms, slugs and snails, snakes, birds' eggs, fruit, and fungi.

© 2004 The Brown Reference Group plc
Printed and bound in U.S.A.
Edited by John Farndon and Angela Koo

Published by:

**An imprint of Scholastic
Library Publishing
Old Sherman Turnpike, Danbury,
Connecticut 06816**

Library of Congress Cataloging-in-Publication Data
Harman, Amanda, 1968–
    Armadillos / Amanda Harman.
        p. cm. — (Nature's children)
    Includes index.
    Summary: Describes the physical characteristics, behavior, and habitats of armadillos.
    ISBN 0–7172–5957–9 (set)   ISBN 0–7172–5958–7
    1. Armadillos—Juvenile literature. [1. Armadillos.] I. Title. II. Series.

QL737.E23H37 2004
599.3'12—dc21

2003049163

Contents

The armadillo is one of the strangest-looking animals on earth, like a cross between a small dog, a rabbit, and a tortoise. When you look at an armadillo, one of the first things you notice is its coat of tough armor. The "armor" is formed by lots of small, hard scales. They are made of the same kind of material that makes up your fingernails and the horns of a cow. The scales are so light and flexible that one type of armadillo can even roll up into a ball.

Armadillos, like this nine-banded armadillo, love nothing more than snuffling around on the ground looking for ants.

Scaly Mammal

The scaly armor of the armadillo looks just like the skin of a reptile, such as a snake or a lizard. Yet the armadillo is actually a mammal. Like all mammals, it has hair—although its hair is sparse and hard to see. Hair grows only on an armadillo's belly and between its bony scales. Like all mammals, too, a mother armadillo feeds her babies on milk from her own body. Last, like all mammals, an armadillo can keep itself at the right temperature even if its surroundings are very hot or very cold.

An armadillo's armor is made of bony bands covered with tiny scales made of hardened skin.

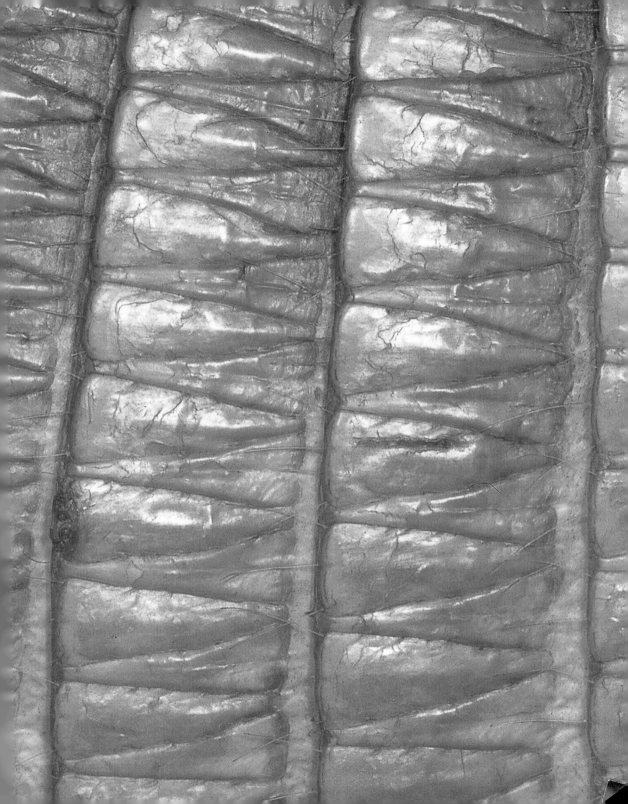

A Mouth Full of Teeth

Scientists group armadillos together with sloths and anteaters, and call them Edentata, which means "toothless." This name is misleading, however, because armadillos are not toothless at all. Edentata are called toothless because they feed mainly on tiny insects and do not have the biting teeth of other mammals. The giant armadillo has up to 100 teeth. Adult humans have just 32 teeth. But all of an armadillo's teeth are very small and not very sharp. Indeed, most of them fall out by the time the armadillos become adults.

The tamandua is a furry, ant-eating cousin of the armadillo that lives in the trees in South America. It clambers slowly and easily through the branches searching for ants, sticking its long tongue into holes in the wood to lick them out.

Fairies and Giants

The 20 types of armadillos all look quite different and come in a wide range of sizes. The smallest is the fairy armadillo. It weighs just 3 ounces (85 grams) and measures 6–7 inches (15–18 centimeters) from head to tail. The biggest is the giant armadillo. It weighs 100–132 pounds (45–60 kilograms) and measures 48–59 inches (122–150 centimeters) from head to tail. Most other armadillos are the size of a small dog or cat.

An armadillo's skin is pinkish brown to dark gray. An armadillo has a long, pointed snout, tiny eyes, and small, upright ears. Its scales stretch in bands from side to side across its back, head, and tail. One armadillo is different, though: The naked-tailed armadillo has no scales on its tail. Some kinds of armadillos are named for the number of scaly bands they have, including the nine-banded armadillo and the six-banded armadillo.

*The six-banded armadillo lives on the grasslands
of South America. It has a very distinctive odor.*

Turtle-Rabbits

Several hundred years ago Central American people called the Aztecs thought the armadillo's scales looked like a turtle's shell. They thought its head and ears looked like those of a rabbit. So they called this strange little animal an *azotochtli*, which means "turtle-rabbit."

Like rabbits, armadillos are very fond of digging in the earth. They dig to find food under the ground, to make their burrows, and to escape from danger. They are very good at digging, because their front legs are large and powerful, and they have long, sharp claws. The giant armadillo has a big middle claw on each of its front feet. This huge claw is the largest in the animal kingdom, up to 8 inches (20 centimeters) long.

Opposite page: Like all armadillos, this three-banded armadillo likes digging. You can see one of the strong front claws it uses to scratch away the earth.

Living in the Americas

Opposite page:
Not everybody likes the nine-banded armadillo. Some people say it steals turkey and quail eggs from farmers. But there is little evidence that this is so.

Different armadillos live in different places in South America and Central America. Nine-banded armadillos are the most widespread species of all. They live throughout most of South and Central America. Some also occur in many places in the southern United States. These armadillos have been spreading slowly northward from Mexico for the last 150 years. They have been seen as far north as Nebraska.

Armadillos can live in most warmish places, but they cannot survive in very dry or very cold areas. They also avoid places in which the soil is too hard for them to dig. The giant armadillo is happiest in savanna grasslands and forest swamps. The nine-banded armadillo can make its home in both tropical forests and cooler woodlands.

Nighttime Wanderers

In tropical countries armadillos hide all day in their burrows to avoid the heat of the sun. They only emerge to look for food when the sun goes down, and it gets cooler. Animals that are active only at night are called nocturnal. Giant armadillos sleep for as many as 19 hours a day.

Armadillos are not very sociable creatures. Instead, they prefer to live by themselves. Sometimes, though, several armadillos of the same sex will share a burrow. The only time armadillos hunt for food together is when a mother goes out with her young babies.

Most armadillos, like this nine-banded armadillo, usually come out after dark. It is cooler at night, and it's harder for their enemies to see them.

Keep off My Patch

Opposite page:
A yellow armadillo standing on its back legs. Armadillos sometimes stand on two legs when fighting off rivals.

Each armadillo has an area of its own called a home range. Night after night the armadillo trots around this area looking for food. Nine-banded armadillos have home ranges anything from 2.5 acres (1 hectare) to 34 acres (13.8 hectares.) Six-banded armadillos may travel even farther. In parts of North America ranges overlap, with several neighboring armadillos living happily nearby.

In parts of South America, however, the armadillos are more aggressive. They fight each other to defend their territories. When another armadillo intrudes, the pair meet face to face, standing up on their hind legs. They then press their tails against the ground to help them balance and lash out with their sharp claws until one armadillo gives up.

Lots of Burrows

Each nine-banded armadillo has up to 12 burrows in its home range. It travels between them during the night and sleeps in a different one each day. Other species rarely use the same burrow more than once.

Each burrow has one main entrance. It may also have several smaller holes for an emergency escape. Sometimes the armadillo blocks up the burrow entrance with plant material before it goes to sleep to keep predators from getting in. Other species, such as the fairy armadillo, use the armor on their backside to plug up the hole.

When the nine-banded armadillo is scared, it doesn't curl into a ball, as some people think. It scurries into its hole as quick as it can.

Cozy Nests

When an armadillo digs its deep burrow, it makes several nest chambers. It lines each with grass and other bits of plants to make them cozy. The armadillo crawls from one chamber to another through long tunnels, up to 25 feet (7.5 meters) in length. To have a handy supply of food, armadillos dig their burrows just below ant hills and termite mounds.

A few armadillos don't bother to dig a burrow. Instead, they move into one abandoned by another animal such as an anteater. The southern three-banded armadillo does this.

Digging a burrow is tiring work. But an armadillo can dig out a huge burrow with amazing speed.

Digging for Food

Armadillos eat a wide range of foods. Many armadillos feed on birds' eggs, nuts, and fruits that have fallen to the ground. Some, like the hairy armadillo, are happy to tuck into the meat of dead animals that they find. They will even burrow underneath a dead animal to get at maggots. Some armadillos eat worms and the roots of plants and fungi, which they dig for with their big clawed front feet.

While they are digging, armadillos grunt and snuffle, with their nose to the ground. As they dig, their hind feet kick away the loose soil behind them. With their snout shoved into the earth so much, you might think that they would choke on soil and dust. They do not, however, because they are able to hold their breath for up to six minutes while they dig.

Eating Ants

Some armadillos eat spiders, grasshoppers, beetles, and caterpillars. Nine-banded armadillos eat even larger animals such as birds, mice, snakes, and frogs. But the favorite food of many armadillos is ants and termites. Both these insects often live in large, strongly built nests in the ground. The armadillos use their powerful legs and sharp claws to tear open the nests. At each meal a single nine-banded armadillo or giant armadillo can collect as many as 40,000 of the juicy little mouthfuls on its tongue. An armadillo's tongue is very long and so wet that ants stick to it.

Armadillos have to eat constantly to stay alive. That is because they are very thin and do not have lots of fat to use for energy when food is scarce.

Quadruplets

Scientists know very little about the way most armadillos breed. Only the breeding habits of the nine-banded armadillo are well known. Nine-banded armadillos mate in the summer. At this time the pair probably share a burrow. Later on they go their separate ways.

The female gives birth the following spring. Then she has four identical babies. They have soft, leathery pink skin when they are born. After just a few hours their eyes are open, and they can walk around. Some other kinds of armadillos take up to four weeks or so to open their eyes and even longer to walk around.

After they have mated, male and female armadillos
often live together for a while.

Growing Up

Armadillo babies are born at a time of year when there are plenty of insects and worms around. That means their mom can eat well and give them lots of milk. So the babies grow quickly. In a few weeks their scales become hard and darker in color. Soon they are big enough to leave the safety of the burrow. Before long they are scurrying out with their mother on trips to find food. After 8 to 10 weeks they stop drinking their mother's milk.

For a while the young armadillos stay with mom. But they often venture out by themselves to find food. Eventually, though, they leave one by one to live on their own. When they are six to twelve months old, they mate and have their own young. In the wild, armadillos generally live for between 12 and 15 years. One nine-banded armadillo in a zoo lived to be 22 years old.

Opposite page:
Young nine-banded armadillos look pretty much like their parents, only smaller. But they cannot look after themselves.

Escaping from Enemies

Opposite page:
For an armadillo this cougar spells danger. An armadillo's armor provides only a little protection against such a big, strong hunter.

Despite their tough armor, armadillos do have quite a few enemies. The biggest dangers are big cats such as cougars and jaguars. Wild dogs such as maned wolves and coyotes can be frightening for an armadillo too. But even foxes, raccoons, weasels, and big birds of prey such as hawks can pose a threat to armadillos caught in the open.

Armadillos living near swamps and rivers have to be wary of caymans and alligators. Those living close to humans are often killed by domestic dogs and cats—or even people who like armadillo meat.

Because they are protected by their armor, armadillos often survive attacks by predators. But they may be badly injured—and so die later because they cannot search for food.

Little Armed One

If an armadillo cannot get away from danger, it has one last line of defense—its armor. This armor is what earned it the name armadillo, which means "little armed one" in Spanish.

The armadillo has no armor on its soft belly—so it must keep it hidden. That is why the nine-banded armadillo presses itself flat on the ground in a tough little hump. The three-banded armadillo rolls itself up in a ball like a hedgehog. With its legs and ears tucked in, the armor plates fit neatly together. The little three-banded armadillo can curl into a ball the size of a grapefruit—tough enough to stop all but the most determined killers. The three-banded armadillo is the only armadillo that can do this.

When threatened, the three-banded armadillo curls up into a tough little ball. The comma shape in the middle is the top of its head!

Running and Screaming

An armadillo's armor is not quite as tough as you might think. It can be badly damaged by the strong teeth and claws of a big cat or wild dog. When danger threatens, most armadillos scurry off—into thick undergrowth or a nearby burrow. The hairy armadillo digs a hole, then firmly wedges itself in. With its feet pressed against the side of the hole and its claws digging in, even the most persistent cat cannot drag it out. The screaming hairy armadillo gets its name because it squeals at the top of its voice when in danger.

When they're running away in fright, hairy armadillos whine and snarl.

Although you can't see through the grass, this naked-tailed armadillo is moving along on tiptoe.

Trotting and Swimming

Armadillos are busy little animals, trotting around in search of food, with their long snout close to the ground. Some species, such as the three-banded armadillo and the naked-tailed armadillo, walk on the tips of their claws. The armadillos' tough armor is not very heavy, and they can get around surprisingly quickly. The scales are also attached to the skin in such a way that the armadillo can bend and turn very easily.

The nine-banded armadillo can actually swim, after a fashion. It's hardly a fish, but it can float very effectively. It sucks air into its stomach to inflate itself like a beachball. That makes it much lighter. Then it paddles with its legs like a dog. If a stream is shallow, the armadillo walks along the streambed, holding its breath until it reaches the other side.

Sniffing out Food

Armadillos have tiny eyes, and they cannot see well when they come out at night to look for food. They cannot even see in color. But their hearing is very sharp. Indeed, when an armadillo hears a sudden noise, it will often leap straight up into the air!

Armadillos find their food mostly by smell. They have a very good sense of smell and can sniff out ants and all kinds of other tasty creatures in pitch dark. The three-banded armadillo can even detect worms 8 inches (20 centimeters) down under the earth.

Armadillos amble around with their nose on the ground most of the time, sniffing for food.

This painting of an armadillo on a rock at Lago a Santa in Brazil is many thousands of years old.

People versus Armadillos

For centuries people have hunted armadillos to eat their meat, which is white and tastes something like pork. Farmers also kill armadillos because they cause problems by digging. An armadillo's digging can ruin crops. The holes they dig can also be a danger to cows, which could trip and break their legs.

To add to the armadillo's problems, people have been cutting down the forests where some live. Several kinds of armadillos are now in danger of dying out completely. The fairy armadillo and the Brazilian three-banded armadillo are both now quite rare.

Helpful Creatures

Many people find armadillos very charming. Texas has even adopted the nine-banded armadillo as its official state animal. Armadillos are also very useful. Their habit of eating lots of insects and slugs and snails makes them very good at getting rid of garden and crop pests. Some people even keep tame armadillos. But they do not do very well in captivity, and it is illegal in some states to keep them as pets.

In some countries people have tried to help the armadillos survive. Today the giant armadillo is protected in national parks and nature reserves in South American countries such as Peru, Brazil, Surinam, and Colombia.

Texans like armadillos so much they adopted them as their state symbol, as you can see on this belt.

Doctor's Helpers

On the warm surface of their paws armadillos sometimes carry the germs of the disease leprosy. This means people can catch leprosy from armadillos if they are scratched, or if they eat armadillo meat that has not been cooked properly. Armadillos are the only animals in the world to carry leprosy germs, apart from people.

In people only the fingers, ears, and nose are cool enough to be infected by the leprosy bacteria. Armadillos have such a low body temperature that the bacteria can grow throughout their body. For this reason armadillos have played a vital role in the struggle to find a cure for leprosy. Thanks to them scientists have a vaccine that they are testing to see if it keeps people from getting leprosy. Nine-banded armadillos have also been used for experiments to help find cures for other diseases.

Words to Know

Burrow A hole or tunnel in the ground where an animal lives.

Extinct When all the animals of a particular species have died, and there are no more left anywhere in the world.

Fungi Organisms such as toadstools and mushrooms that belong to the kingdom Fungi.

Habitat Part of the environment in which a particular animal usually lives.

Mammal A warm-blooded animal that is covered by hair or fur and feeds its young on its own milk.

Mate To come together to produce young.

Nocturnal Active at night.

Predator An animal that hunts and eats other animals for food.

Reptile Any cold-blooded animal that is covered by scaly skin and lays eggs.

Species A type of animal or plant.

Temperate Places on the earth with a climate that is not very hot and not very cold.

Territory An area where an animal hunts or breeds. The animal generally defends its territory against other animals.

Vaccine A liquid that is injected and used to protect people or animals from disease-causing germs.

INDEX

Cover Photo: Ardea: Piers Cavendish
Photo Credits: Ardea: Steve Hopkin 7, Keith & Liz Laidler 29; Bruce Coleman: Antonio
Manzanares 34, Hans Reinhard 33; Corbis: Theo Allofs 38, Pierre Colombel 42, Macduff
Everton 41, Philip Gould 45, Harvey Martin/Gallo Images 4, Steve Kaufman 37; NHPA: Palo
Haroldo 20, Jany Sauvanet 12; Oxford Scientific Films: Bob Bennett 15, Fabio Columbini 11,
Paul Franklin 30, Joe McDonald/AA 16, Partridge Films Ltd. 26/27, Konrad Wothe 8; Still
Pictures: Roland Seitre 19, 23.: Ardea: Piers Cavendish.